THE KEY

THE KEY

Reflections and Wisdom of a New England Carpenter

Peter Cassels-Brown

iUniverse, Inc.
Bloomington

The Key
Reflections and Wisdom of a New England Carpenter

iUniverse books may be ordered through booksellers or by contacting:

iUniverse
1663 Liberty Drive
Bloomington, IN 47403
www.iuniverse.com
1-800-Authors (1-800-288-4677)

ISBN: 978-1-4759-3797-8 (sc)
ISBN: 978-1-4759-3799-2 (hc)
ISBN: 978-1-4759-3798-5 (ebk)

Library of Congress Control Number: 2012912877

Printed in the United States of America

iUniverse rev. date: 08/09/2012

Contents

Photo Courtesy of Linda Blair

ACKNOWLEDGMENTS

While I have tried to the best of my ability to use my own words to express the thoughts embodied in this book, the thoughts themselves belong not to me but to all of us. They come to us from a place beyond time and space and have been expressed by many people in many different ways over thousands of years. I feel, though, that there is always room for one more attempt to capture their essence and boil them down into a concise format that is both engaging and digestible. We do not need a book that is either long or complicated to remind us of what we already know in our hearts. It is my hope that this book can serve as such a reminder when we forget, and as such, offer some comfort and maybe even some insight into the beautiful adventure that is our collective life and evolution.

At this point it would be impossible for me to pick apart a half century of reading and conversation in order to credit every word that has served to remind me of our true nature. Instead, I wish simply to list those individuals who have each in their own way contributed to my understanding of what it really means to be human in relation to the cosmos from which we come. I apologize in advance to anyone I may have left out.

Kahlil Gibran
Fritjof Capra
Brian Swimme
Stephen Hawking
Rumi
René Dubos
Deepak Chopra

Jerry and Rene Russell
Dr. Richard Alpert/Baba Ram Das
Don Miguel Ruiz
Rhonda Byrne
Wallace D. Wattles
Robert Spieler
Bob Dylan
Eckhart Tolle
Carlos Castaneda
Wayne Dyer
Andrew Cohen
John Dickason
Alastair, Rosemarie, and Elisabeth Cassels-Brown

INTRODUCTION

It feels as if I have been looking for something all my life. I have caught fleeting glimpses of it from time to time. These glimpses are always accompanied by a pulse of energy and joy, just enough to get my attention, as if to teasingly say, there is more where that came from.

Recently, even amid huge challenges that life has presented to me, these glimpses have happened more frequently and have lasted longer. The times of struggle and pain between the glimpses have become sparser and shorter lived. In fact, it almost seems that the challenges themselves have been the catalysts that have accelerated a growing peace, strength, and joy. Indeed, on some level, what doesn't kill you makes you stronger.

When circumstances become overwhelming and unbearable, my ability to resist them eventually fails, and by default I find myself surrendering to the moment (not the circumstances). It is in this moment of acceptance and nonresistance that a feeling of warmth creeps in to places that have been numb or in pain, and a profound peace displaces the turmoil, tension, and anxiety. Given a chance, this peace, in turn, morphs into a joy that can hardly be contained.

It is my hope that in the following pages I can share some of the thoughts and reflections that have contributed to and emerged from this transmutation of pain and fear into peace and joy.

We live in an exciting time when a growing number of people are remembering wisdom that has always been there but was hidden from all but a few for so long. In this shift lies my optimism and hope for a better world. A better world is possible if enough people believe it. I feel we are approaching a critical mass where this can happen. It has started already. We are on this journey together, and maybe I will meet some of you along the way.

REVELATION

*So often times it happens that we live our lives in chains,
and we never even know we have the key.*

—Eagles

Revel-ation
Rev-elation
Revel-elation

Neither heaven nor hell is an actual place, separate from the universe we know, but that does not mean they don't exist. Both of them are present here and now, and we have a choice regarding which one we are in.

It was a beautiful day in March (which historically can be a slow time for us). I had decided to take a few ski runs at Sugarbush on my way to work. When I got to the mountain, the sun was already shining brightly in a chrome blue, cloudless sky. It was reflected even more brilliantly by the white crystal beach of corn snow that lay on a few surviving trails, while, all around, vegetation stirred and began to awaken from its winter slumber. As the temperature rose to over seventy degrees, my heart leapt with joy at being in the right place at the right time for once. A few runs later, however, thoughts of work started to creep into my mind. They were thoughts of phone calls, paperwork, placing orders, setting up projects, meeting with clients, service calls, etc. I started to feel guilty that I was having so much fun on a workday.

I decided to check my phone calls and e-mail when I realized I had left my cell phone at home. I became uncomfortable thinking about missed communications and possibly irritated clients. More guilt.

I had a choice. I could pack it in and head to the office and take care of business, after all, that had been the original plan, or I could stay for another run or two. I decided that another run wouldn't hurt. Then another. And another. Okay, time to go to work; then I ran into a friend. Okay, one more. Mmm. This weather and this type of snow are rare. Okay, one more. It's two thirty, and time to go; there's still time to take care of things . . .

As I walked past the lodge on my way to the parking lot, a band was playing on the Castlerock Pub terrace (on a Thursday in late March, at 2:30 p.m., when there are only a few people around?)—not just any band, but a local favorite, an extremely good band that I hadn't seen in ages. Okay, hang out for a tune or two . . . mmm, well, I am thirsty. Just one beer, a couple more tunes . . .

At 5:00 p.m. I actually left to go to work. I did make contacts and organize the next day after all, but the truth is, it could have waited until the next day. Days like the one I just described happen only a few times a year if I am lucky. I was there, but I almost missed it. Fortunately, I was present enough not to have missed it, and was profoundly grateful for that, but definitely had tortured myself unnecessarily.

Another time, we were taking advantage of unseasonably warm weather (above freezing) in February to get the jump on a spring project by pouring the foundation in the dead of winter. Risky, but the alternative was being unemployed.

Long story short, the water table was higher than anticipated for that time of year, which created numerous challenges for us, such as a three-foot-deep freezing pond where the foundation needed to go. The drainage was impeded by the existing house, which was to be moved onto the new foundation. Pumps helped until the temperature dropped to significantly below freezing. We did manage to successfully pour the foundation, but I found myself alone at 2:00 a.m. in a frozen, muddy trench resembling a World War I foxhole. As I wrestled with frozen equipment in the wee hours of the morning, all the while resembling a frozen mud rat, I surprised myself by laughing out loud at the absurdity of it all. At the same moment a wave of warmth and gratitude swept over me for a few reasons. First, I actually had work at a time when many people, especially builders and carpenters, did not. Second, it made me appreciate my own fortitude, for which I was hugely grateful in the moment. Finally, it was the sense of some unaccountable old joker just laughing his ass off to witness my predicament. In that presence, I could not help but laugh at myself and the situation.

The point of all this is that we can be in a situation that would seem to be as close to heaven as is possible in our human world, yet still torture ourselves with anxiety, tension, and stress. We can also find ourselves in a situation that truly resembles hell, yet transcend it to experience joy, gratitude, and love of life.

Our circumstances are external, but our experience of them is internal. We have a choice of how to respond to any given situation. Our choice of response not only determines how we feel about ourselves and the situation, but since the world functions as a mirror for us, it also determines to a large degree the outcome of those circumstances.

GRATITUDE

Giving thanks for the blessings we do have is grounding, healing, uplifting, and energizing. By focusing on the best things, we attract more of that to us.

It can help pull one out of a tailspin when things are looking bleak, spirits are sinking, and fear is creeping in. The beneficiary of gratitude is the giver of thanks. Giving thanks feels good.

Gratitude creates a healthy energy through and around you. People can't see it, but they can feel it. It helps make a person feel comfortable around you (because it helps you to be comfortable with yourself), which improves the chance of successful interaction.

When I'm feeling anxious, tense, or stressed, nothing gets me back on track like thinking of the things I have to be grateful for. I start with the basics, such as shelter, clothes, food, my children, work, etc. I keep going until I get to a point where I'm feeling quite fortunate indeed. It is hard to be in a negative space when you are truly grateful. When one is in a positive, grateful space, circumstances, seemingly almost by magic, have a way of changing to a more positive situation.

Many times at work, when I focus on the challenges I face as a business owner in an uncertain economy, I feel overwhelmed by the liabilities and obligations. I start to panic, and wonder how I will ever make ends meet. That is inevitably when circumstances seem to conspire to support and fuel that fear.

If I change my focus, however, and think about all the resources I have amassed in the last several decades, and the opportunities that are right in front of me, and give thanks for those, in a heartbeat I feel wealthy already. It seems like the most natural thing in the world that things will progress in a positive direction. In fact, I can't really see it any other way. Inevitably, this is when I will get a phone call from someone who wants us to help them with a really good project, is interested in investing in an expansion of our business, or is offering us an opportunity that supports that expansion.

Gratitude has the power to change my energy completely, from anxiety about how I am going to balance the budget to excitement about all the possibilities that exist for me. When my energy changes, there is a corresponding shift in what happens externally. When I am anxious, that is when I get calls from customers with warranty work, or we have equipment or vehicle issues, all of which cost me money. When I am grateful for what we have and am feeling upbeat and confident, that is when customers call in with exciting new projects that will bring in enough money to take care of any expenses we may have and much more.

FORGIVENESS

Holding anger toward another person, it has been said, is like holding on to a hot coal with the intention of throwing it at someone. All the while you are the one getting burned.

Like gratitude, forgiveness benefits primarily the forgiver. It is not as much to exonerate the perpetrator of a violent act, crime, or injustice, as it is to free the victim from toxic, angry feelings, and to help them move forward into their own healthy space.

Forgiveness is empowering for the forgiver. Without it, a tendency is to fall into victim head. Nothing is more disempowering than to claim the victim space. Even if one has been horribly wronged, it only makes matters worse to wallow in victimhood. To blame someone else (even if justified) is to give away power. To forgive is to claim power.

I have had opportunities recently to put this into practice, and the results are nothing short of profound. The difference between feeling anger and bitterness versus acceptance, forgiveness, and love is like night and day. Anger and bitterness eat away at you and are simply the worst feelings in the world. To accept what is, and to extend love to that, is to give yourself the gift of a free heart, unencumbered by the poisonous drama of resentment. I am not talking about the righteous anger that is born of injustice and inspires action to facilitate justice. Nonetheless, even with that, what is important is the healing action and the justice, not the anger.

Forgiveness is absolutely essential if one is to be truly free.

Without boring you with the details of personal drama, suffice it to say that a few things have happened over the years in the areas of work, friendship, and love that were absolutely gut-wrenching and tore me apart.

Whenever I had let myself go to a place of being a victim, or a place of blame, the ensuing flood of emotions was absolutely crushing, toxic, and incredibly destructive (internally, that is; I wasn't throwing things or taking it out on anybody else directly). Fortunately, these feelings were so intolerable that I could not remain in that space for long. If I had remained there, I am certain it would have literally killed me one way or another, be it cancer, heart attack, stroke, car accident, etc.

It seemed the only answer was to accept what was, forgive what I felt was unjust, and extend love to those who were involved. The alchemy of this was simply amazing. No sooner than I managed to turn my feelings around, the world around me responded with compassion, support, and opportunity. The rotten, heavy feelings of anger and resentment were displaced by the lighthearted feelings of joy and freedom as the world once again opened up to me with new opportunities on every level.

LOVE

Similar to gratitude and forgiveness, the real value in love comes in the power of giving. The receiver of love is truly blessed, but the real joy in love is found in the giving. Loving unconditionally is devotion. For thousands of years, devotion has been recognized as a path for the spirit in its quest for union, or unity consciousness.

Love is a master key that can unlock almost any door.

Love and fear do not readily share the same space, somewhat like oil and water.

So often we sabotage ourselves by letting our insecurity and fear get the better of us, whether it is in the context of work, relationships, friendship, marriage, etc. The world reflects back to us what we feel inside. If we are anxious, circumstances will mirror and feed that anxiety or fear. The fear can displace the love.

If we can nurture the joy and warmth of love inside us, the world will reflect that back in the form of people and circumstances that support more of that. If we can keep our internal love fires lit, and they are reflected back to us by the world, we begin to lose the feelings of duality and separateness that alienate us and cause suffering. We become suspended in a field from within and without, and find ourselves swimming in an ocean of love. In this way, love displaces fear. When we are in this place, anything seems possible. Our dreams take on a dimension of depth and solidity. They become alive and three-dimensional. This further fuels an undercurrent of joy as we realize we can ultimately create anything we want. Indeed, we begin to understand that perhaps that is why we are here.

The choice is ours—to live separately and in pain, or to live in unity and love. Simple? Yes. Easy? Not always. It takes constant stoking of our internal love fire to maintain this vibrantly healthy space.

The thing to remember is that separateness or duality is just an illusion. By definition, we are all made of the same stuff, and that is all there is. Whether we like it or not, we are all connected at the most elemental level, the seamless energy that is the universe.

As life progresses, naturally there are losses along the way. How one regards those losses can make a huge difference to the quality of one's life. If one focuses on the loss of love or a loved one, the sadness can seem unbearable at times. If one focuses on the love that was there in the first place, that is something that can never be taken away. In a way it is like an Olympic medal. Whether you have the medal itself or not, nothing can take away the fact that you won it. It will always be a part of you, and in that way it is never truly lost. It adds richness of texture and color to the fabric of our lives. It stretches us and helps us to grow, and if we allow it, it opens us to the next level of life.

UNION

Albeit the illusion of separateness is a stubborn one, at least when viewed from our normal perspective of the world as we see it, namely, what you see is what you get. There is, however, more to life than meets the eye.

One need look no further than to the field of subatomic physics, or quantum theory, to see that this is true. It is a most rigorous and disciplined field of science based on physical observation and mathematics. It is interesting that in such a technical, factual area of study, we come closest to actually seeing the magic of the universe we live in.

Atoms, long considered the building blocks of our physical world, are primarily empty space and are in constant motion. Comprised of a nucleus (a proton) and orbiting particles (electrons), an atom resembles a solar system with vast amounts of empty space between these components (99.99 percent empty space, to be precise). These components are further broken down into subatomic particles. Upon close inspection, these particles appear to behave rather strangely. Again, that is if they are viewed from our normal frame of reference, that of the physical world as we see it. They appear to blink on and off like lights on a buoy on the ocean or a lake at night. Now you see them, now you don't. Just because you can't see them doesn't mean they aren't there. At this level, they respond to the way in which they are observed or measured. If the observer chooses to measure a particle as a physical entity with a specific mass, location, direction, and velocity, that can be done. If the observer chooses to measure the entity as a wave, that is to say they can predict where it will be at a given time (a probability amplitude) that also can be done. This is to say that how the particle behaves depends on how the observer chooses to measure it. In other words, they are inseparable. This is the interface between the observable world as we know it and the realm of pure energy from which all things are made. When our reality is viewed from this perspective, it becomes clear that the universe is a single seamless entity.

Why, then, does it not feel like that most of the time? Determining that is one of the fundamental challenges we all share.

To know this truth experientially in one's heart has been the goal of spiritual traditions since they were established thousands of years ago, and probably for individuals long before that. It remains central to the challenge of finding out who or what we really are.

I have been fortunate (I use this word loosely) to have a number of experiences that have brought this home to me. One that sticks in my mind was a night (March 9, 1978, to be precise; I will never forget it) when my friend Ted and I decided to walk across Lake Champlain from Burlington, Vermont, to Plattsburgh, New York, at midnight, a distance of twelve miles one way across the ice (of course, that meant we would have to walk back as well). I won't bore you with technical details, but suffice it to say we were perhaps not in possession of our best judgment at that time. We got nearly to the center of the lake (already more than five miles offshore), when we simultaneously stopped in our tracks without saying a word to each other. We realized that the ice was moving up and down on the water and that the St. Lawrence Seaway was flowing openly in front of us only steps ahead. The current was surprisingly rapid, and the ice, with our weight, was starting to tip in the direction of the midlake river. Water was moving up the ice shelf toward us as if to invite us to join it in its travels to Quebec. At that moment, I looked up for an instant at the clear black sky with its millions of stars reaching for the horizon like an internally lit crystal chandelier, and a thought occurred to me: If I slip into this stream and am swept under the ice, part of me will not survive. There is another part, though, that may not even go below the ice, but simply merge with the stars. This happened in a split second but was one of the most powerful experiences of my life. I was absolutely convinced beyond any shred of doubt that there is a dimension to our being that is indestructible, infinite, timeless, and incredibly beautiful.

"Ted?" I said.

"I know," came the reply.

Without another word, we carefully backed up until we felt we were no longer on a water-covered ice slide into certain infinity. We turned around and began to retrace our steps back to Perkin's Pier, over five miles away. There were scattered snowdrifts along the way with our footprints in them that we used as trail blazes to keep us on track, as the lights of Burlington were so spread out that it was hard to determine where we had started from. We both shed a layer of clothing and tied it around our waists as we commented on how warm it was. As we wended our way, we began to realize that, in places, ice we had walked out on had started to turn to water. We had to circumnavigate numerous soft spots and water holes along the way that had not been there on our way out. A strong, warm south wind was literally eating the ice. About four silent miles later, still more than a mile offshore, we again both stopped on the same footstep. We were looking ahead over an area of clear black ice with no cracks or air bubbles that could tell us how thick it was. We had instinctually stopped, as it started to feel as if we were walking on water. I got down on my hands and knees, and looked across the ice toward the lights of Burlington, in hopes of being able to determine the thickness of the ice. Nothing. I raised my hand and punched the ice, hoping to feel some solid resistance upon contact. My hand went right through the ice without hesitation, and a low geyser of water began to rise up through the hole. Cracks started to radiate out in all directions from where we stood accompanied by the sound of breaking eggshells. Now we could see the lights of Burlington reflected in the cracks of the ice like lightning bolts beneath our feet. Indeed, it felt like plugging oneself into a light socket.

We separated by at least fifty feet to distribute our weight, but the cracking continued, and we felt a sinking feeling as the ice started to give way. I had another split-second vision, which was that even if the ice started breaking, if I could just move fast enough, it would be breaking behind me but not beneath me. I said, "I weigh nothing," and with the same silent synchronicity that had stopped us on the same footstep, we both started bolting toward shore, Perkin's Pier now securely in our sights. Never before or since in my life have I moved so fast. I swear the ice was breaking with every step, but by the time it gave way, I was already onto the next foot, and so was Ted. Even as we approached the thicker ice near the breakwater by the pier (probably a foot thick at that point), we did not slacken our stride until we were both standing on terra firma. Even once on solid ground, I wasn't sure I was actually going to live. My heartbeat was over two hundred beats a minute, and I thought for sure I was going to drop dead of cardiac arrest.

As we gradually regained our composure, we noticed an International Scout (one of the original SUVs) heading out toward the ice to retrieve an ice fishing shanty, as this definitely appeared to be the last chance to do so. We ran over to meet it as it gingerly eased itself onto the solid ice within the breakwater. We told the driver that we did not think it was good idea. He looked at us as if we were deranged (perhaps we were). He proceeded on as we watched. As he went beyond the breakwater, we saw brake lights, reverse lights, and then no lights. We strained in the darkness to see a silhouette of a vehicle on the ice but could see nothing but the lights of Burlington reflecting off the ice into the darkness beyond.

With a sick feeling in our guts, but still too shell shocked to go back out onto the ice, we went over to the Coast Guard station on the other side of the pier and reported that we thought a vehicle had gone through the ice by the breakwater. Then we went home.

The next morning, on the front page of the *Burlington Free Press*, was a picture of a large crane at Perkin's Pier, reaching out over the ice, its cable ushered by Coast Guard frogmen pulling the Scout out of the water. Apparently alerted by our warning, the driver had been driving with his window open and had managed to escape before his vehicle sank to the bottom of the lake. There was also a picture of a few people on a piece of the ice shelf that had broken loose and drifted out into the lake, who were being retrieved by a helicopter equipped with floodlights.

We walked down to the lake a little later to survey the scene. Miles of what had been ice that we walked on the night before were now open water. The wind had started to create swells that broke up the ice, and the warm temperature had rapidly digested the ice as it broke up. What was left had been swept by the Saint Lawrence northward.

The point of all this is that sometimes life will take us to the edge to show us the dimension of ourselves that is beyond time and space. Once you have been there, there is no turning back. You will never be the same. In that place, no doubt remains concerning the unity of all that is.

THE CONNECTION

This unity is the premise upon which the use of the word *manifest* as a verb, i.e., "to manifest," is founded. Our minds being inextricably linked to an infinite web of energy and intelligence (the womb of creation) gives us the power to create our own reality and is the cornerstone of personal responsibility.

We are responsible for the world we create for ourselves. This is both liberating and at times intimidating. It is satisfying and uplifting to own our successes, but it can be a bitter pill to own our failures, injuries, and illnesses. Without ownership, though, we have no power to improve a situation or to heal an injury or illness. In the case of catastrophic injury or terminal illness, ownership can at least empower us to find peace, if nothing else.

Why do "bad" things happen to "good" people and "good" things happen to "bad" people? Life can seem at times not to be fair in that way.

In unity consciousness there is no good or bad. What is just is. The values we apply to any given situation judge it as good or bad. Of course, anger, pain, and sadness can surround accidents, injuries, illness, death, divorce, and tragedies of any kind. Something can happen, though, when life becomes unbearable, if we choose to accept the opportunity and responsibility presented to us in the moment. It is a process akin to alchemy, the legendary art of turning lead into gold. In this case it is the transmutation of pain, fear, and suffering into freedom, creativity, and joy. It is using the energy in any given situation to fuel our own evolution.

How does this happen?

Life will push us to the limits of endurance if only to make us "let go."

Of what?

Fear, tension, and anxiety. The stronger we are, the more we hold on, the greater the challenge life will serve up to make us let go.

We surrender.

To what, or whom?

The moment.

It is in this "letting go" that we discover our true nature. It is like standing barefoot on a sandy beach and leaning slightly into the steady sea breeze as we absorb the rhythm of the pounding surf. It is wordless and totally enveloping.

Zoe 3rd grade ink drawing of bamboo

THE GREAT SPIRIT

*You lose yourself; you reappear; you suddenly find you
have nothing to fear . . . .*

—Bob Dylan

How people define god is subjective and semantic. He/she/it can be so
many different things to so many different people, yet it is but one thing.
All spiritual traditions are ultimately paths to the same mountaintop.
By definition there can only be one god. That is, if you define God as
omnipotent, omniscient, and benevolent—the energy, intelligence, and
love that make up the entire universe. There are problems with this
definition, however. When it comes to being omniscient, omnipotent, and
benevolent, it would seem you could only have two out of three. God can
be omniscient and omnipotent but not benevolent (otherwise there would
not be so much suffering). It can be omniscient and benevolent but not
omnipotent (otherwise there would not be so much suffering). It can be
omnipotent and benevolent, but not omniscient. (Catch my drift?). These
considerations can move one to a more decentralized concept of God.
God is not so much a separate entity as it is the intelligence, energy, and
love that is in all things. To say "God created man in his own image" is to
say that we emerged from the omnipresent intelligence and gave it form.
That intelligence manifests itself in us and is an integral part of us.

The challenge before us is to remove all barriers that prevent us from
experiencing this miracle in all its glory. It is not so much about finding
a consciousness that is new or separate, as it is about uncovering one
that has been here forever, and will be forever more. It is our collective
consciousness; it is what we are made of. In this sense, we are truly the
heart and mind, eyes and hands of God. We are the universe aware of

itself, the eyes of the world. We are coevolving simultaneously with the universe as it unfolds in its own growth process. Each and every one of us is a creator. Our mission is to fully grasp this reality and live it.

To say God is not a separate entity is not to say that God is no entity at all. There is a spirit, a presence that is all pervasive. It is powerful yet playful, creative yet destructive, peaceful yet restless, loving yet seemingly sometimes even angry. It is the spirit from which we are fashioned. It is our spirit. It is who we are. We are coevolving simultaneously with it. To discover this spirit as our essence, our being, our awareness, is to discover our infinite core.

Religions at one point may have served to help us find or define this spirit, but over time they have evolved into tools or strategies for controlling the masses. As such, they can be more of a hindrance than help when it comes to our evolution. The premise upon which they operate is that individuals who discover their real power are dangerous, as they present a threat to the status quo. Nothing could be further from the truth. The only risk is to those who would use fear to control others.

The value I see in religions, or spiritual traditions, as I prefer to call them, is their ability to build community and to draw people together. A lot of good can happen when people support each other and work together to relieve suffering of their fellow man, such as hunger, illness, pain, and unrest.

Some of the essential teachings (the ones that have not been manipulated, twisted, or misinterpreted) of these traditions still serve as timeless wisdom that can help us to find our way. Still, it is up to the individual to see through the layers of dogma to discover the essence of the teachings, and to apply them the way they were intended by their original authors. Very often, the teachings are in the form of a metaphor, and there can be some danger in interpreting them too literally. In fact, there have probably been more wars fought and people killed in the name of God than for any other reason (greed would probably come in a close second, and both could fall into the category of fear). This violence, born of fear, ignorance, and intolerance, stems mostly from extreme fundamentalist interpretations of writings that may bear little resemblance to the original teachings.

I also have a bit of a problem with us all being miserable sinners by default. We didn't ask to be here, and most of us are making the best of it in our own way, in many cases creating beautiful lives full of love, light, and creativity. Many of us are still struggling but are evolving in our own way at our own pace. That does not make us sinners.

There are differences between God, religion, and spiritual practice.

God, the Great Spirit, Allah, or whatever one chooses to call it, is the living presence in all that is. It is the life energy, the intelligence, the love, and the creativity that is the spirit of the universe.

Religions are man-made structures, rules, and organizations, created to maintain order. At best, they can provide community and a well-traveled path to the common spiritual mountaintop, but it is still up to the traveler to find his or her way. At least he or she has some company along that way. At worst, religions are about control and manipulation, and are full of hypocrisy.

Spiritual practice is the exercise or discipline of aligning oneself with the Great Spirit to the point of realizing it as our own. However we choose to do that, whether in a group/organization/religion or alone, is our choice, and, in my mind, all are equally valid. Whatever works for you is fine.

Ultimately, it is the realization of our true selves, of our essential nature, that matters.

HAPPINESS, HEALTH, AND PROSPERITY

No one is a failure who is enjoying life.

—Salada tea bag

Nothing succeeds like success.

—Old proverb

Success is a moving target. It can mean different things at different times to different people. To me, success means not just surviving but thriving. Success is waking up in the morning, excited just to be alive, eager to embrace the day.

It is difficult, however to be in this place unless your basic needs of food, shelter, clothing, and love are met.

Happiness, health, and prosperity are three sides of an equilateral triangle that are interdependent. If any of these three components are seriously lacking, the other two are, at least to some degree, compromised.

The Buddha would say, focus on being happy now, first and foremost, and health and prosperity will follow. That might be difficult if you are wondering how you will shelter, cloth, and feed your children. A Western business executive might say just the opposite—take care of business, and happiness and health will follow (that is, of course, unless he/she is a Buddhist). It's sort of the chicken or the egg thing.

What is the door through which we are to realize the abundance of the universe? The answer is simple, and has been said by many people in many different ways. That, however, does not make it easy.

The only thing you have ever had, and the only thing you will ever have, is this moment. The past is history; the future is a projection. Granted, the past has brought us to this point, and thus has something to do with the thoughts, feelings, and patterns of behavior we call ourselves. It is not who we are, however. This is an important distinction. Who we are ultimately is beyond the constraints of time and space.

Similarly, the hopes, dreams, and goals we call the future have a direct influence on the plans we make and the actions we take to realize them. The future, nonetheless, is only a projection. Any hoping, dreaming, planning, or action happens now, in this moment. It is what we think, feel, dream, and act on in the present moment that shapes our future. This is the door.

If your present moment is fearful or anxious, then you will attract situations that reflect that fear and anxiety. If your present moment is filled with happiness, confidence, and love, then you will experience situations that reflect those feelings.

Happiness, health, and prosperity are about taking responsibility for what we are thinking and feeling internally, knowing that the external world to a large degree is a reflection of the internal one. It is also about having a clear vision of what it is we want, accompanied by the unwavering faith that the vision is in the process of becoming reality, and about giving thanks for it as if it is a sure thing. Finally, the rubber meets the road when our actions in the present moment are aligned with our vision, and we wholeheartedly give it our best shot. We are then fully alive, and can be at peace with ourselves, and live without regrets.

Photo, courtesy of Buzz Kuhns photography

THE KEY

The essence of all that exists is found in present-moment awareness, consciousness in its purest form. This awareness can displace fear, anxiety, pain, and suffering. Fear and anxiety are constructs of the mind. Pain and suffering are responses to those constructs. As darkness gives way to light, anxiety and fear give way to present-moment awareness. Suffering is like static caused by a bad ground connection. To ground oneself in present-moment awareness, or consciousness, is to remove that static.

When you shine the light of your consciousness/awareness on the darkness of your fear, anxiety, tension, and pain, the darkness gives way to the light as night does to the dawn. Duality and separateness give way to unity as all becomes one, all becomes light.

This oneness is ever present, but most of the time we create the illusion of separateness, of duality, from which all pain and suffering arise. When we dissolve this illusion by grounding ourselves in the present moment (presence), our fear and discomfort (dis-ease) vaporize.

In this place of being peacefully grounded in present-moment awareness, one can become aware of an ever-present undercurrent of joy. This energy fuels our evolution, or growth, and propels us forward on our path toward the realization of our dreams. This is true happiness, health, and prosperity.

The challenges of everyday life can continue to stir up feelings of fear and anxiety, but now we have a powerful tool for pushing them back and making the space for the ever-present creative energy that is the force that can turn dreams into reality.

Listen to your heart, and have the courage to believe what it is telling you, and have the strength to act on it to the best of your ability. These are simple words, and have been said many times in many ways, but they are true.

Your brain is a transceiver that broadcasts a signal that travels to the farthest limits of the universe, not unlike a stone cast into a still pond, which causes ripples that go all the way to the shore. The primary difference is that it does this instantly, not limited by time or space, and does not diminish with distance.

While I believe it was Albert Einstein who first said, "Thoughts are things," it has been echoed by so many people that I have to admit I am not certain. It has also been scientifically proven that thoughts can influence physical objects (i.e., water), and thus can influence the world that is external to our brains. Long before that, the Buddha said, "All that we are is a result of all that we have thought." Ultimately, for better or for worse, we get what we focus our thoughts on.

More precisely, our thoughts/feelings vibrate at a frequency that attracts people, things, and circumstances that match that frequency. This has been generally labeled in contemporary literature as the law of attraction. We create and receive that which we think and feel—the stronger the feeling, the stronger the signal. Our dreams and fears manifest themselves equally readily in relation to the intensity of our feelings connected to those dreams and fears.

In the simplest terms, if we can manage to ground ourselves in present-moment awareness and love (in other words, feeling as good as we possibly can at any given moment), then we will attract those people, things, and circumstances that vibrate at that frequency, and that will ultimately support our happiness, health, and prosperity.

This is *the key*.

LETTING GO AND
LIGHTENING UP

Richie Havens opened up for a show I went to see one year that was part of the summer outdoor concert series at Stowe's Spruce Peak. At one point he got somewhat philosophical and shared this nugget of wisdom. He said he had been feeling a bit down for a while and had decided to take the bull by the horns. He said, "I got up one morning and said to myself, 'I'm not going to let anyone or anything get me down today.' And you know what? It worked. That is some powerful shit!"

"It's a slow turning, from the inside out . . . but you come about . . . John Hiatt

It is probably fair to say we have witnessed more change and evolution (much of it technological) in the last century than at any other time. Transportation, communication, and information availability are evolving at an accelerating rate.

While this is exciting, it also has created challenges for us in terms of being responsible for the consequences of this growth. We need to balance the development of technology with our health, the health of the planet, and the integrity of our relationships with each other as individuals, cultures, and nations.

This is a huge responsibility. For many of us, just surviving each day and keeping our own life together seems huge enough by itself. Moving beyond our individual challenges and struggles in order to advance our collective evolution will require additional energy, focus, and commitment.

All too often our creative energy is locked up in our daily concerns and survival challenges. To allow this energy to flow more readily, we need to let go of our fear and lighten up! A good sense of humor is essential to this end.

While we may have perfectly valid reasons for being fearful (the threat of injury, illness, financial struggle, etc.), it is important to note that fear simply doesn't help. In fact, fear is probably responsible for more heart attacks, cancer, strokes, and murders than anything else. Fear is a killer, pure and simple. Letting go of fear makes room for the creative energy we need to move forward in a positive, productive way.

It may seem at times that you are really at the end of your rope, hanging on for dear life. The tendency is to hang on until you cannot hang on any longer. Then you fall . . . about an inch or two, and find yourself standing on the ground. You realize you are still here, and are okay. Whatever the problem was may still exist, but somehow you can see it from a different perspective and, more often than not, find a way to work it out.

I suggest (unless, of course, it is an actual physical rope you are hanging from) that you let go proactively. It is much easier to work on almost any situation when you are standing on the ground as opposed to hanging on for dear life with all your might.

When we recognize the tension we are holding, and the energy it is wasting, we are able to let go of it with a tangible sense of relief. This frees up a tremendous amount of energy that can be used to move us forward.

Sometimes we are paralyzed by fear, but by letting go of it, we regain freedom of movement.

I remember going to a Stevie Wonder concert in Boston at the height of the bussing experiment in the late sixties or early seventies. The idea of bussing was to enhance cultural diversity and level the educational playing field by transporting students from one district to another to better distribute available resources and break down discrimination. It seemed like a good idea on paper, but in reality it created a huge amount of racial tension with a certain amount of violence accompanying it.

The concert was almost canceled, as it seemed the perfect venue for a riot, and authorities were afraid people would get hurt or even killed. The show, however, did go on. The tension was so thick around the Boston Garden you could cut it with a knife. In fact, that was exactly what the authorities were afraid of. Right at the beginning of the show, though, Stevie Wonder came out and addressed the crowd. He asked if any children were present. When he got the response that there were, he asked that one white child and one black child be brought up onstage. As he is blind, the children were brought to him, and their hands were put in his, one on either side of him. Holding their hands, Stevie looked straight out into the crowd and said, "I can't tell the difference."

That was the end of the problem, at least for that night. The concert went off without incident. All of the raw energy present in the house fueled a spectacular show that was appreciated by one and all. When it was over, it was almost surreal how peacefully the crowd disbursed amid smiles and the occasional exchange of "Peace, brother."

It was all about getting people to let go of their fear, and it worked.

WHERE TO GO FROM HERE

Before enlightenment, chop wood, carry water. After enlightenment, chop wood carry water.

—Zen proverb

The traditional concept of enlightenment is that of a spiritual master retreating to a cave on a mountain or some other remote location in order to have uninterrupted access to "the one" or universal unity consciousness. Once enlightened, then this person returns to share the wisdom he or she has received and now embodies. The enlightened ones become gurus (teachers) in order to train their disciples or students.

An ancient Zen philosophy is that as a being becomes fully realized or actualized (enlightened), he or she does less and accomplishes more, until ultimately he or she does nothing and accomplishes everything. For millennia in India whole villages have grown around these spiritual masters, who themselves appear to do nothing.

There was a time when just the recognition of this state of mind seemed to be enough. Times have changed. The world is a busy, noisy, place and there is a lot of work to be done. Participation is required. Everyone who is able needs to roll up his or her sleeves and get to work. The need for internal peace and present-moment awareness is greater than ever, but the average person does not have the time and money to retreat in order to become fully actualized. Trying to "achieve" enlightenment in this bustling world might feel at times like trying to change a tire at 80 mph. *The key* is to know that what we are looking for is always there, all around and inside us. All we need to do is let go of resistance and fear, and surrender to the moment. This is easier said than done, but it is simple and is something we can do on the fly. In fact, it is something we must do as we move through our daily work, activities, and interactions with others. As a species we cannot afford to leave self-realization to the masters. We need as many fully realized beings as soon as we can possibly have them if we are to survive and thrive before it is too late.

We are all coevolving at one level or another with the universe itself. Indeed, we are the eyes and hands of the intelligence, creativity, and energy that constitute all that is. The universe needs us to participate in its unfolding and evolution. It does not stop expanding, growing, and changing to evolve. It does not retreat. It charges on in a way that says there is no turning back. We are caught in this unfolding whether we like it or not. To resist it is to resist the entire universe. The moment we resist it, we experience pain, suffering, frustration, discontent, etc.

When we accept the present moment without resistance or judgment, we enter the flow, and all of the energy of the universe propels us forward.

An example of present-moment acceptance, becoming unstuck and entering the flow comes, to mind.

It was St Patrick's Day in Tuckerman Ravine. The sun was trying to poke through the clouds, but it had been snowing for days, and nearly everything was closed due to avalanche danger. My friends, frustrated after carrying about ninety pounds each of ski gear, clothing, food, and drink into the Hermit Lake shelters in anticipation of fresh tracks and the steep and deep, decided to ski back down the Sherburne Trail, to go skiing where trails would be open at one of the nearby ski areas.

I decided to stay. As everything in the bowl was closed, I left my skis at the shelter and headed up Lion's Head ridge with crampons and an ice ax. The snow was midthigh deep, but the ridge was too steep for snowshoes, so it was easier to just plow through. In a couple of hours I was on the summit of Mount Washington, alone, a rarity. I savored having the mountain to myself, and strolled down to the ridge along the top of Tuckerman Ravine.

A stiff wind came up, and was creating and destroying snow sculptures before my eyes. The snow would catch on the uneven surface of the ridge (jagged rocks and ice, stripped by the wind, poking up through the snow) and would build up into a snowman as if by magic. The next strong gust would annihilate this new being, and it would disappear in a cloud of snow over the edge of the bowl.

The wind continued to get stronger until it had to be going somewhere around eighty miles an hour. The sun was starting to move to the backside to begin its descent into late afternoon, so I decided it was time to head back down to the shelter. At that moment, an exceptionally strong gust lifted me slightly off my feet and blew me toward the lip of the bowl like the snowmen I had been watching. It dropped me right at the edge of the lip, which was by now a massive cornice of wind-packed powder. The cornice gave way, and I started to slide with it. I spun around and dug my crampons and ice ax into the hard crust where the new snow had slid off. I watched the snow go over the edge like a waterfall.

My landing had created a fault line across the top of the lip. I tried to go back up, but there were now several feet of new snow hanging over my head where the cornice had been. Going back would be impossible. I looked over toward Lions Head. I started to traverse the lip, digging in my crampons and ice ax, with my back to the bowl. It was a lot of work, and Lions Head started to look farther away than it seemed earlier. I was starting to get hungry and tired, and the sun had disappeared over the ridge. I looked at the snow in the bowl and thought, open or not, skis would be the right tool for the job. Oh well. I turned around and faced out with the ridge at my back and looked at the massive amount of snow in the bowl. I've heard it said that an inch on the summit can equal a foot in the bowl when the wind is blowing it all off the surrounding ridge and into the ravine. It definitely seemed to be the case that day.

I realized resistance was futile. I thought about it for a minute, and then hunger, fatigue, and the setting sun got the better of me. I took one step into the bowl, and the headwall let go at the fracture line I had created. It is eight hundred vertical feet from the lip to the bottom of the bowl. Five steps later (about 150 vertical feet each), I was being spit out onto the bottom of the bowl, where the avalanche was compressing itself into densely packed powder. Fortunately, I was on top of it, having ridden it down. I stumbled, trying not to impale myself on my ice ax. I caught myself and regained my balance and stood there for a few minutes amid the settling snow cloud and the thunder from the avalanche that was still echoing around the bowl.

Years later, when Shawn Colvin wrote her song, "Riding Shotgun Down the Avalanche," I could relate.

I dusted myself off and, realizing I was none the worse for wear, made my way back to the shelter for a cup of hot tea (and a good stiff cocktail).

Shortly thereafter, I was paid a visit by the ranger on duty, who turned out to be a friend of mine. She said, "Was that you?" I confessed that it was. She proceeded to read me the riot act, mostly out of loving concern for my well-being, stating that she did not want to see my name added to the list of people who had not been as fortunate as me, on the wall in the Pinkham Notch lodge at the bottom of the ravine. I knew a couple of people on that list, and had to agree with her. She told me to never do anything like that again. I tried to explain that I didn't do it on purpose, but my appeal fell on deaf ears.

It was like many moments in life when you might want to go back or resist going forward but can't. When you try, you are met with huge resistance, like that of an impenetrable cornice hanging over your head. When you face straight ahead and accept the moment, you are swept along with all the momentum of the universe. In this case I was lucky, but, still, the universe got me back to the shelter in the fastest, most efficient way possible, in time for tea.

Photo, Dick Smith, Tuckerman Ravine, courtesy of New
England Ski Museum

LIVING THE DREAM

There's a longing deep inside our hearts, and no one will tell us why.

—Michael O'Keefe/Bonnie Raitt

Whatever you can do or dream you can, begin it. Boldness has genius, power, and magic in it.

—Goethe

You only see the world you make.

—John Hiatt

What we all need beyond our basic survival requirements is inspiration. Without it, our daily life seems flat and meaningless. This inspiration can come in many forms. Many times it is our love for our children, family, and friends that pushes us on through our daily challenges and keeps us going when we might otherwise give up.

Each of us at some level has a dream waiting/wanting to be realized. This dream, more than anything, defines the essence of who we are. That dream is our individual manifestation of the universal/cosmic intelligence and creativity that constitutes all that is. It is our link to the divine, as it is the divine energy attempting to live through us. This is the source of inspiration that can lift us up beyond our daily struggles. It is the energy that fuels us in our evolution and creates the added dimension that gives meaning to our lives. It is the fuel that keeps our love fire burning.

At times, our dreams may seem distant, unreachable, and unrealistic. Nonetheless, if we keep at least one eye on our dreams as does the captain of a ship on his compass, we may surprise ourselves in the end when those dreams come true. At the very least, our lives will be richer for trying.

Reaching for something in the future, while staying fully present here and now, reminds me of hiking through the jungle in Kenya in 1978.

Four of us embarked on a ten-day trek into the Loita Hills armed with the only map made of the area at that time. The British army had surveyed it in 1958. The map was simple, with five-hundred-foot contour lines as the primary feature. If two lines were close to each other, you could probably interpret that as a cliff. Also, a few clearings and water holes were noted. Generally the clearings were near water holes as they were primarily created by elephants, water buffalo, and wildebeest. The only trails were created by animals, and generally followed the ridges, except when they went to the water holes, and were not on the map. No one lived in the jungle, and, in fact, the locals thought we were crazy for going there, especially to stay overnight, several days walk from the surrounding open grasslands where they herded their goats and cows. These days, they have a growing tourist industry with guides and marked trails and, I'm sure, updated maps.

We set our sights on one of the clearings as our destination for the first day, as it would have room for our tents and a water hole nearby. At least it was there in 1958.

We got to a clearing that looked just about right in terms of size, shape, and proximity to water. The only thing that didn't seem right was that we got there hours ahead of schedule. Giving ourselves the benefit of the doubt, we made camp and celebrated what seemed to be a good day of hiking.

The next day, we broke camp and set out on our way. It wasn't long before we came upon another clearing almost exactly like the first one.

An hour down the trail, there was another one, then another one, and so on. Only one was on the map in that area. By late afternoon, we were starting to wonder a little bit about our location. We each had a copy of the map (in case anything happened to the others, such as becoming lion food, etc.). We separated, and each tried to figure where we were on the map given our topography, landmarks, and estimated distance traveled. When we reconvened to compare notes, we were all about ten miles apart from each other. We were only on our second day, and had already rendered our maps somewhat obsolete. My friend Dave said, "It's okay, we're not lost, we just don't know where the fuck we are."

We did notice a landmark, however, with a note by it. Apparently, in 1958, an army Land Rover had driven across the high grassland at a time when the ground was wet and soft, and had sunk in significantly, leaving tire tracks deep in the clay soil. Subsequently, there had been a drought, and the tire tracks had been baked into the clay, and to some degree were preserved. The tracks ran north/south, and our route was basically east/west. We figured if we walked due west for about seven days, we would hit the tire tracks. We would be able then to follow them south to the village where we planned to meet another group.

We agreed to a compass bearing, and set off saying that we would stay on that bearing no matter what. We had been warned, however, of a mass of magnetic rock somewhere in the vicinity that could seriously mess with a compass. Of course, we had the sun, which in the end, was the most reliable, except that around midday, it was directly overhead (being near the equator), which was not all that helpful.

Almost immediately we encountered our first obstacle, an understory of six-foot-tall nettles as far as we could see, north, south, and west, filling the space between the trees and vines. We were wearing long pants and long-sleeved shirts for protection already, so we marched bravely on into the venomous weeds. The oil in these nettles is very similar chemically to bee venom. As it started to penetrate our clothes, it stung. Not knowing what else to do, we forged on and finally emerged on the other side, looking like we had all hiked through a giant beehive. Fortunately, no one was allergic to bees.

A couple days later we approached a few of those contour lines that were kind of close to each other to find a fifteen-hundred-foot cliff that wrapped around us, again to the north, south, and west. We had no choice but to backtrack for hours, to where the topography softened enough to be able to climb down to the watering holes, around the cliff, and back onto our bearing.

Eventually, on the seventh day (nine days total), we emerged from the jungle into the grassy plains. It was the better part of another day before we came across what looked convincingly like tire tracks. They had eroded with decades of rain and sun but were still recognizable.

We ambled south along the tracks until we came upon a village where we met up with our friends, right on schedule (give or take a few hours).

The point as it pertains to living the dream is this; though it may be a long and winding rocky road to get to your dream, if you set your bearing and stick to it, chances are you will get there, one way or another. If you don't get there, at least you will have peace of mind, knowing that you tried.

Photo Courtesy of Linda Blair

FORTUNE COOKIE WISDOM

Here are a few words the universe chose to send me via the random wisdom of fortune cookies over the years. They are random indeed, and several remain to be seen. Nonetheless, they are somewhat encouraging, so I am sharing them with you as random affirmations of positive thinking.

You are kind and friendly.

Versatility is one of your outstanding traits.

He who hurries cannot walk with dignity.

You will be fortunate in everything.

There is a prospect of a thrilling time ahead for you.

Time is the wisest counselor.

You have a quiet and unobtrusive nature.

You are heading in the right direction.

Your dearest dream is coming true.

Working hard will make you live a happy life.

You are original and creative.

The Key

You and your wife will be happy in your life together.

The current year will bring you much happiness.

You will spend old age in comfort and material wealth.

You should be able to make money and hold on to it.

Your life will be happy and peaceful.

You are a practical person with your feet on the ground.

You will inherit a large sum of money.

A PERSONAL AFFIRMATION

Here is a personal affirmation I wish to share at the risk of being too personal. I have always been an open book, though, so here it is.

Following the end of a marriage that I thought surely would last forever, I found myself, after a time, in the uncharted waters of the online personals. With my self-esteem shattered and still in more pain than I thought was humanly possible, I had to pull myself together if I had any hope of perhaps being able to start over with someone new. The ad requested a catchphrase/paragraph that summed up who you are, to head the ad. I struggled with that a bit, but this is what emerged.

I had to ask myself,

Who am I?

What is my essence?

Me

I work hard; I play hard.
I'm tough as nails and soft as silk.
I have a heart of gold.
I'm patient and steady, strong and kind.
I'm creative, innovative, and gutsy.
I'm honest and fair.

I thought, is that really me? It was as if it came from beyond, as my mind was drawing a blank. The more I thought about it, I realized it was more me than I knew. The Samurai say there is a part of us that water cannot wet, fire cannot burn, and weapons cannot cleave. That is the part that is tough as nails and soft as silk, and it is in all of us. It is who we are at our core. It is part of the beauty of being human.

ABOUT THE AUTHOR

Peter Cassels-Brown is currently owner of Mountain Woodworks/Green Mountain Renewable Energy, a custom design/build/renewable energy company in Bristol, Vermont. He studied solar design at the University of Vermont and went to Woodbury College for graduate studies in mediation. He currently lives in Bristol with his two children.